☑ **W9-ASC-080**

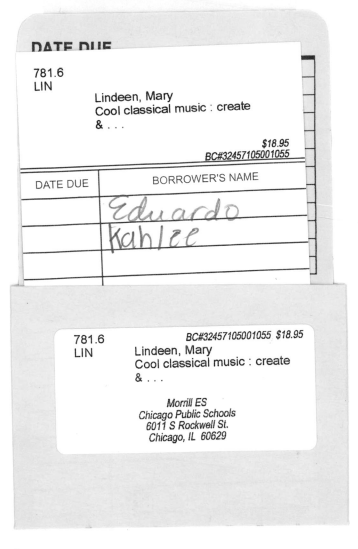

DATE DUE

781.6
LIN

Lindeen, Mary
Cool classical music : create
& . . .

$18.95
BC#32457105001055

DATE DUE	BORROWER'S NAME
	Eduardo
	Kahlee

Cool CLASSICAL MUSIC

Create & Appreciate What Makes Music Great!

Mary Lindeen

ABDO Publishing Company

Visit us at www.abdopublishing.com

Published by ABDO Publishing Company, 8000 West 78th Street, Edina, Minnesota 55439. Copyright © 2008 by Abdo Consulting Group, Inc. International copyrights reserved in all countries. No part of this book may be reproduced in any form without written permission from the publisher. The Checkerboard Library™ is a trademark and logo of ABDO Publishing Company.

Printed in the United States.

Design and Production: Mighty Media, Inc.
Photo Credits: Anders Hanson, iStockphoto/Diane Diederich, iStockphoto/Terry Wilson, Jupiterimages Corporation, Photodisc, Shutterstock
Series Editor: Pam Price

Library of Congress Cataloging-in-Publication Data

Lindeen, Mary.
 Cool classical music : create & appreciate what makes music great! / Mary Lindeen.
     p. cm. -- (Cool music)
 Includes index.
 ISBN 978-1-59928-969-4
 1. Music appreciation--Juvenile literature. I. Title.

 MT6.L74 2008
 781.6'8--dc22

                          2007040741

Note to Adult Helpers

Some activities in this book require the help of an adult. An adult should closely monitor any use of a sharp object, such as a utility knife, or perform that task for the child.

Contents

The Music Around You

Did you ever get a song stuck in your head? Maybe you just couldn't help singing it out loud. Sometimes a song reminds you of a day with your friends or a fun vacation. Other times a tune may stay in your mind just because you like it so much. Listening to music can be fun and memorable for everyone.

We hear music everywhere we go. Music is played on television shows and commercials. There are even television stations dedicated to music.

Most radio stations play one type, or **genre**, of music. Some play only country music. Others play just classical music. Still others play a mixture of different kinds of rock music. Just pick a kind of music that you like, and you will find a radio station that plays it!

The different genres of music have many things in common, though. They all use instruments. Some instruments are played in many different types of music. The differences are in the ways instruments are played. For example, the drumbeats are different in various music genres.

Some kinds of music have **lyrics** that are sung by singers. Did you know that the human voice is often referred to as an instrument?

Playing music can be as fun as listening to it! Every person can play a part in a song. You can start with something simple, such as a tambourine. You could then work your way up to a more difficult instrument, such as a drum set. Remember, every great musician was once a beginner. It takes practice and time to learn how to play an instrument.

With music, one of the most important things is to have fun! You can dance to it, play it, or listen to it. Find your own musical style and make it your own!

A Mini Musical Glossary

classical music – a type of music from Europe that began centuries ago as the first written church music. Today it includes operas and music played by **orchestras**.

country music – a style of music that came from the rural parts of the southern United States. It is based on **folk**, gospel, and blues music.

hip-hop music – a style of music originally from New York City in which someone raps lyrics while a DJ plays or creates an instrumental track.

Latin music – a genre of music that includes several styles of music from Latin America. It is influenced by African, European, and native musical styles. Songs may be sung in Spanish, Portuguese, or Latin-based Creole.

reggae music – a type of music that came from Jamaica in the 1960s. It is based on African and Caribbean music and American rhythm and blues.

rock music – a genre of music that became popular in the 1950s. It is based on country music and rhythm-and-blues styles.

The Classical Music Story

Most people think classical music is serious music. It is true that writing, singing, or playing it well takes years of practice and study. But anyone can listen to and enjoy it anytime. Learning a few of the basics will help you appreciate what you're hearing even more.

The Middle Ages (470s to 1400s). It is hard to say exactly when and where classical music started. Most experts agree that it has its roots in Europe. The first written classical music comes from Christian monks who used chants as part of their worship. Also during this time, traveling performers went from village to village. They sang **folk** songs, played instruments, and recited poetry.

1300

1600

The Renaissance (1300s to 1500s). Gradually, church services began to include hymns that ordinary people sang. More people learned to read and write, so more people wrote songs and composed music. Artists painted richer, complicated paintings. Architects designed complex buildings with lots of decorative features. As people became more educated, more writers wanted to share their ideas.

The Baroque Period (1600 to 1750). Music from this time was usually written for royalty, rich people, and the Christian church. This was mostly because no one else could afford to pay the **composers**. The music was very fancy and complicated. In fact, some of the music was so complex that many musicians couldn't even play it! Famous baroque composers include Johann Sebastian Bach, Antonio Vivaldi, and George Frideric Handel.

The Classical Age (1750 to 1820s). Composers began to write music that was easier to play and more enjoyable to hear. Music was written not just to impress people but also to make them happy and relaxed. **Orchestras** had more musicians and instruments. The musicians needed a conductor to keep everyone playing at the same speed. Famous composers from this period are Franz Joseph Haydn, Wolfgang Amadeus Mozart, and Ludwig van Beethoven.

The Modern Era (early 1900s to today). Classical composers continue to look for new ideas and new sounds for their music. They borrow ideas from folk music, **jazz**, blues, and new technology. They write music for new instruments. They experiment with new ways to play old instruments.

Some modern era music sounds a lot like the music that came before. Some sounds very different from music anyone has ever heard. Famous modern composers include Igor Stravinsky and Claude Debussy. For the first time, this group also includes Americans, such as Aaron Copland, George Gershwin, and Leonard Bernstein.

1900

The Romantic Period (early 1800s to early 1900s). Composers began writing about love, fantasy, and magic. This music needed even larger orchestras to play it. Musical instruments were now being made by machine instead of by hand. All of this resulted in music that was full of drama and passion. And it was played more loudly and with more notes.

More and more people liked listening to classical music. Composers didn't have to worry about writing music only for wealthy people. Richard Wagner, Pyotr Ilich Tchaikovsky, Johannes Brahms, Franz Liszt, and Gustav Mahler became famous composers during this time.

Pyotr Ilich Tchaikovsky

What Is Classical Music?

When some people hear the term *classical music*, they think of powdered wigs and harpsichords. Or they are reminded of stout women singing loudly while wearing Viking helmets. But those who know better know that there is much more to classical music than that.

Instrumental Music

Some classical music is written for instruments only. It includes many combinations of musicians and instruments.

solo – one instrument.

duet – two instruments.

trio – three instruments.

quartet – four instruments.

chamber ensemble – any small group, usually two to ten players.

symphony orchestra – a large group of 50 to 100 or more musicians.

Vocal Music

Music written for the human voice is called vocal music. In many classical compositions, vocal music is often combined with instrumental music. These are some kinds of classical vocal music.

sacred music – songs to be sung in church, including chants, masses, and hymns.

chorus – songs for a mix of voices, from soprano to bass.

opera – a funny or dramatic story told using both vocal and instrumental music.

Timbre

No, this doesn't mean that classical music can make trees fall down. *Timbre* simply means that different instruments and voices make unique sounds. For instance, you can easily hear the difference between a note played on a piano and the same note played on a flute. You can also hear the difference between the sound of a woman's voice singing and the sound of a man's. This different quality of sounds is timbre. Sometimes this is also referred to as tone color.

An **orchestra** has many different kinds of instruments in it for a reason. **Composers** use them to create specific musical effects. For instance, it works better to have trumpets play loud, strong marching music. For soft, gentle music, it sounds better to have an instrument such as the flute play the main part.

Operas also take advantage of timbre to make memorable music. A man with a very low voice, a bass, often plays an evil or frightening character. The quality of his voice creates a scary mood. An innocent or sweet character is often played by a woman with a very high voice, a soprano. The tone color of her voice matches a lighter, more likable character.

Emotion

Great classical music creates strong emotions in those who listen to it. Classical music might make you feel sad, joyful, calm, or excited. It doesn't matter what the emotion is. What matters is that you feel the emotion deeply when you listen to the music.

Many classical music composers never became famous. Their music was technically correct. But, it didn't connect with the emotions of the people who heard it. The famous composers wrote music that touched the listener's emotions.

Harmony

Playing two or more notes at the same time creates harmony. These can't be just any notes, though. The notes have to sound good together. Classical music composers are very skilled at creating harmony, or knowing which notes will sound good together. Harmony makes music sound full, or rich with sound. A full, rich sound is one very noticeable feature of classical music.

Rhythm

The rhythm of music is like its heartbeat. It is the pulse of the music. The rhythm might be fast, slow, or somewhere in the middle. To let musicians know what **tempo** to play, classical music composers write special instructions in Italian when they write the music.

prestissimo – very, very, very fast.

presto – very, very fast.

vivace – very fast.

allegro – fast and lively.

moderato – moderate, or medium, pace.

adagio – sort of slow.

lento – slow.

grave – very slow and serious.

largo – very, very, very slow.

Classical Instruments

In a **symphony orchestra**, musicians who play instruments from the same family usually sit together. There are four main families of orchestral instruments. They are strings, **woodwinds**, brass, and **percussion**. Keyboards are often used as well.

Strings

violin

viola

cello

bass violin

harp

Woodwinds

piccolo

flute

clarinet

oboe

English horn

bassoon

Brass

trumpet

French horn

trombone

tuba

Keyboards

piano

harpsichord

pipe organ

Percussion

xylophone

cymbals

tambourine

snare drum

timpani

bass drum

wood blocks

triangle

chimes

Classical Greats

A lot of classical music has been created over the centuries. In fact, it's hard to know where to start listening! These are some well-known classical compositions and artists.

Great Composers

- Johann Sebastian Bach
- Ludwig van Beethoven
- Leonard Bernstein
- Johannes Brahms
- Aaron Copland
- Claude Debussy
- George Gershwin
- George Frideric Handel
- Joseph Haydn
- Franz Liszt
- Gustav Mahler
- Wolfgang Amadeus Mozart
- Arnold Schoenberg
- Johann Strauss
- Igor Stravinsky
- Pyotr Ilich Tchaikovsky
- Giuseppe Verdi
- Antonio Vivaldi
- Richard Wagner

Great Classical Works

- Mass in B Minor, by Bach
- Symphony no. 9 "Choral," by Beethoven
- Violin Concerto, by Beethoven
- Symphony no. 5, by Beethoven
- *Appalachian Spring*, by Copland
- Symphony no. 9 *From the New World*, by Dvorak
- *Messiah*, by Handel
- *Requiem*, by Mozart
- Piano Concerto no. 2, by Rachmaninoff
- *The Four Seasons*, by Vivaldi

Great Opera Singers

- Marian Anderson
- Kathleen Battle
- Maria Callas
- José Carreras
- Enrico Caruso
- Placido Domingo
- Marilyn Horne
- Jenny Lind
- Jessye Norman
- Luciano Pavarotti
- Leontyne Price
- Paul Robeson
- Beverly Sills
- Joan Sutherland

Great Musicians

- Chee-Yun, violin
- Van Cliburn, piano
- James Galway, flute
- Vladimir Horowitz, piano
- Yo-Yo Ma, cello
- Wynton Marsalis, trumpet
- Itzhak Perlman, violin
- Isaac Stern, violin

Great Operas

- Bizet
  Carmen
- Mozart
  The Marriage of Figaro
- Puccini
  La Bohème
  Madama Butterfly
  Tosca
  Turandot
- Rossini
  The Barber of Seville
- Verdi
  Aïda
  Falstaff
  La Traviata
  Macbeth
  Otello
  Rigoletto
- Wagner
  Tristan and Isolde

Great Conductors

- Vladimir Ashkenazy
- Daniel Barenboim
- Leonard Bernstein
- Arthur Fiedler
- James Levine
- Zubin Mehta
- Neville Marriner
- Seiji Ozawa
- Robert Shaw
- Georg Solti
- Leopold Stokowski
- Arturo Toscanini

Music Production

The way music is recorded makes a big difference in its final sound. The type of microphone used and where it is placed are very important. The **acoustics** in the recording room are critical.

Recording music is a difficult process. That is why most classical music is recorded in recording studios. A recording studio has professional recording equipment. It also has soundproof rooms. Studio engineers place the microphones and run the equipment.

Once the music is recorded, it needs to be worked with to bring out the best sound. This is mostly done with computer programs or mixing boards that help separate the sounds. This process is called mixing.

This sound engineer is using a mixing board.

Downloading Music

At one time, music could be bought only at record stores. Today you can buy music by downloading it onto your computer from a Web site. You can then put the downloaded music onto an MP3 player.

Sometimes people violate **copyright** law when they download music. Copyright law helps musicians get paid for their music. Some illegal Web sites let people download music without paying. You need to make sure you are downloading music from a legal Web site. Otherwise, you could be breaking copyright law.

It is also important that you get permission from an adult before downloading music. When you download music, you are charged a fee. Make sure an adult knows how much the music costs. And make sure an adult knows the Web site you are downloading from.

Record Collecting

Many people collect vinyl records. Music stores sell new and used records. You can also find used records at garage and estate sales. Many **audiophiles** prefer the sound of records. They believe the sound is warmer and truer than the sound of CDs.

Experience Classical Music

Recorded Music

The easiest way to hear classical music is to listen to it on the radio. The pieces played on classical music stations are often sections of longer works. This allows stations to play music that appeals to a wide range of classical music fans.

You can also hear classical music on television. Some shows broadcast entire **concerts** or operas. Sometimes these are recordings of live public concerts. Sometimes the performance is done especially for television.

Classical music is often used as the soundtrack, or background music, in movies. The next time you go to a movie, listen for classical music. Pay attention to how it helps set the mood.

Live Music

A church is one convenient place to hear live classical music. Many hymns and choir **anthems** sung today were written by classical **composers** centuries ago. The music played before and after the service is often by these composers too.

If you go to the ballet or take ballet lessons, chances are you've heard classical music. Some famous classical music, such as Tchaikovsky's *Swan Lake* and *The Nutcracker*, was written for the ballet.

Almost every city and town offers live classical music concerts. You might hear local artists perform. Or, visiting singers and musicians may perform.

16

Famous Concert and Opera Halls

Where you hear classical music has a lot to do with how it sounds and how it makes you feel. For instance, an **orchestra** can sound completely different when it plays in a small concert hall rather than a large one. And, the audience for each concert is different too. It changes according to who is playing or where the concert is. This is why many fans of classical music like to attend performances in different cities when they travel.

Musikverein

Vienna, Austria
www.musikverein-wien.at/startseite.asp

Along with Boston's Symphony Hall and Amsterdam's Concertgebouw, this is considered one of the finest concert halls in the world. It opened in 1870 and is home to the Vienna Philharmonic Orchestra. It is known for its excellent **acoustics**.

Symphony Hall

Boston, Massachusetts
www.bso.org

Symphony Hall opened in 1900. The Boston Pops and the Boston Symphony Orchestra perform there. The hall is considered one of the best in the world because of its wonderful acoustics. Its long, narrow, high shape helps to focus the sound toward the audience.

Sydney Opera House

Sydney, New South Wales, Australia
www.sydneyoperahouse.com

The Sydney Opera House opened in 1973. It is one of the most recognized and photographed buildings in the world. The white "sails" that make up its roof complement its setting beside Sydney Harbor.

Carnegie Hall

New York, New York
www.carnegiehall.org

Built in 1890, this is one of the most famous concert halls in the United States. Until 1962, it was home to the New York Philharmonic. Today it hosts classical and popular music concerts along with lectures, classes, and more.

Metropolitan Opera House

New York, New York
www.metoperafamily.org/metopera/

The Metropolitan Opera Association, or the Met, is the largest classical music group in the United States. The Metropolitan Opera House has been its home since 1966. The Metropolitan Opera House is located in Lincoln Center for the Performing Arts.

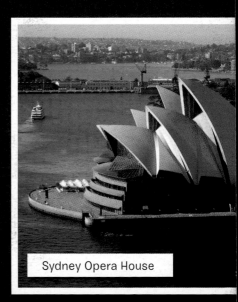

Sydney Opera House

Make Your Own TROMBONE

Materials Needed

- a plastic, cardboard, rubber, or metal tube about 2 to 3 feet (61 to 91 cm) long. The **diameter** should be small enough that you can seal the end of the tube when you press it against your mouth.

- a second pipe of the same material and length but with a larger diameter. It should slip easily over the first tube.

In Italian, *tromba* means "trumpet," And, *trombone* means "big trumpet." Trombones are brass instruments. However, you can make your own trombone out of plastic, cardboard, rubber, or metal. All you need are two tubes, and you're ready to make music!

How to Play a Mouthpiece

1 To play a trombone, the musician blows into the mouthpiece. Your trombone won't have a separate mouthpiece, but you will use the same technique to play your trombone.

2 Place one end of the smaller tube against your lips, keeping your mouth closed. Stretch your lips out to the sides of your face, as if you are trying to flatten your lips against your teeth. Imagine making a straight line with your mouth.

3 Now blow air through your closed, stretched lips. Your lips will vibrate a little as the air is forced through them into the tube. Practice blowing into the end of the tube until you can make sound come out if it.

4 Now stretch your lips even tighter. It might be more difficult to blow, but it will make your trombone sound a little higher. Now loosen your lips just a little and blow again. This should make your trombone sound a little lower.

CLEF NOTES

You will make a better sound with your trombone if you keep your cheek muscles tight when you play. Don't let your cheeks puff out when you play.

How to Use the Slide

1 The larger tube will be the slide on your trombone. Hold the smaller tube with one hand, and slide the larger tube right over it. Start at the bottom and slide it toward the top.

2 Hold the slide about halfway down the length of the smaller tube while you blow into the mouthpiece of your trombone. How does it sound?

3 Move the slide tube almost to the bottom and play a note. Be careful not to send the slide shooting off the end of your trombone! How does it sound now? Now move the slide tube almost to the top and play a note. What do you notice about this sound?

Experiment With Sound

1 You can play many different notes with your trombone. It all depends on how tightly you stretch your lips when you blow and where you hold the slide. The possibilities are endless!

2 Blow continuously into the trombone while you move the slide. Start at the top and slide down to slide from a high note to a low one. Now do the opposite and slide from a low note to a high one.

3 Use different lengths of tubes. Make a trombone that's only a foot (30 cm) long. It will play very high notes. Make a trombone that's five feet (1.5 m) long. It will play very low notes. You might need a friend to help you handle the slide!

4 Hold a small cup or bowl over the bottom end of the slide as you play. This is called using a mute. How does this change the sound?

CLEF NOTES

The higher the slide is on the trombone, the higher the notes sound. The lower the slide is, the lower the notes sound.

Classical Music
RHYTHM

Materials Needed

- something to tap a beat with, such as hands, feet, wooden spoon, drums, cymbals, triangle, castanets, or gong
- radio
- notepad and pencil

Hold your fingers on a pulse point on your body, such as your wrist or the side of your neck. Is the pattern of your heartbeat going bump-BUMP, bump-BUMP? That repeating pattern of beats is the rhythm of your body. Each song has its own rhythm too. In classical music, the rhythm in a song might be very clear and simple, or it might be very complicated and tricky to find.

Step 1

Listen to any kind of music on the radio station of your choice. First, just try to clap, march, bang, drum, or thump to the beat you hear.

Step 2

Now try to write the rhythm you heard. You can use words or think of your own way to write it down. You might try using symbols or simple patterns. The important thing is to think of a system that you can use later to repeat the same rhythm.

Rhythm

*** / *** / *** / ***

1, 2, 3 — 1, 2, 3 — 1, 2, 3 — 1, 2, 3

A-b-b, A-b-b, A-b-b, A-b-b

Step 3

Now tune the radio to a classical music station. Listen to several songs and practice first tapping and then writing out the rhythm for each one.

Step 4

Turn the radio off. Write some rhythms of your own.

Step 5

Practice your rhythms. Play them again and think about the answers to these questions.

What kind of dance or movement might match each rhythm that you wrote?

How does each rhythm sound when you tap it slowly? How does it sound when you tap it fast?

Are your rhythms easy or complicated?

Which is your favorite?

Two Classic Classical Rhythms

A **march** is one kind of classical music with a strong, steady rhythm. The beat matches the pattern of walking feet. The rhythm of a march is easy to hear, which makes it easier for members of a band or military unit to keep their steps together. You can write the rhythm of a march like this, ONE-two, ONE-two, ONE-two.

A **waltz** is a kind of classical music written for ballroom dancing. Like a march, the rhythm of a waltz is easy to hear, which helps the dancers keep their movements in step with each other and with the music. Waltz rhythm has three beats, with the emphasis on the first beat. You can write it like this, ONE-two-three, ONE-two-three, ONE-two-three.

Dancing the waltz

Write a
CLASSICAL SONG

Just as there are many different kinds of classical music, there are many classical song styles. Some of the oldest songs come from sacred music, including chants and hymns. **Folk** songs, especially those from older European countries, are often considered classical music. The most famous classical songs come from the opera, which is basically a good story that has been set to music.

Materials Needed

- notebook and pencil
- tape recorder or computer with recording capability
- an instrument

Classical Lyrics

1 Song **lyrics** usually have several verses. The verses do the main work of telling the story. Most songs also have a chorus, or a set of words that repeat throughout the song. The chorus is usually repeated after every one or two verses. The chorus often highlights the theme of the song.

2 Think of a story you want to tell. Or pick a story someone else has already told that you would like to put to music. Many classical songs began as poems, religious writings, or historical tales. Later, someone else turned them into songs.

3 Make some notes about what parts of the story you want to include in your song. These are just quick notes to help you later when you write the song. Also think about the main idea or theme of your song. Write down some options for the chorus. For this first songwriting project, try to keep your song to two or three verses.

4 Start writing! You can write either the verse or the chorus first. Some writers like to tell the story and then summarize the most important idea in the chorus. Other writers like to write the chorus first, so they can emphasize the theme of the song.

Classical Melody

The melody is the tune of your song, or the way the music flows from note to note. How do you make a melody? Let us count the ways!

1 Find some inspiration. Hum some notes that come to you as you reread your lyrics silently. You might find the melody that suits your song this way, almost by accident.

2 Once you've picked the melody, start fitting the lyrics to it. Or fit the melody to the lyrics. There is no right way to do this! Use one part of the melody for the verses and another part for the chorus.

3 Practice singing your lyrics to your melody. Make recordings so you can listen to the way it sounds when it's all put together. Make changes until you are satisfied with your song.

Classical Rhythm

Every song needs a beat that sets its pace. Now that you have **lyrics** and a melody, the rhythm of your song should almost fall into place!

1 First experiment with some different rhythms. Try beating a drum or tapping the table in different ways until you find the right speed and the pattern.

2 Record all the rhythms you try on a tape recorder or a computer. That will make it easier to pick your favorite later.

Put It All Together

1 First, get the rhythm of your music going. Tap your foot to the beat of your song. Or, have a friend play the beat. It's really hard for one person to sing, play, and drum!

2 Next, play the melody of your song on an instrument. Keep practicing. It may take a while before you can play and keep your foot tapping.

3 Now, add the lyrics. Sing the words while you tap the beat and play the notes.

Dance the WALTZ

The waltz has been around for over 300 years. It began as a European **folk** dance. Today the waltz is still a popular ballroom dance. When it is done well, the waltz is elegant and beautiful.

Step 1

Face your partner. The boy puts his right hand on the girl's waist. He holds his left arm up, with the palm facing his partner. The girl puts her right arm up and rests her hand lightly in the boy's left hand. The girl's left hand is on the boy's right shoulder.

Step 2

On the first beat, the boy takes a sliding step forward with his left foot. At the same time, the girl takes a sliding step back with her right foot.

Step 3

On the second beat, the boy slides his right foot forward and to the right. At the same time, the girl slides her left foot backward and to the left.

Step 4

Between the second and third beats, the boy shifts his weight from his left foot to his right. The girl shifts her weight from her right foot to her left. But, don't move your feet!

Dance Floor Dos and Don'ts

Always move in a counterclockwise circle around the outside edge of the dance floor. This keeps all dancers moving in the same direction. It is safer, and it makes everyone look better.

Always look over your partner's shoulder as you dance, especially if you're the leader. This will help you see where you are going. It also makes the two of you look better.

When you lead, make sure your partner doesn't bump into anything or anyone. She's dancing backward, after all! When you're really good, you and your partner will be able to turn in your own small circles as you circle around the dance floor.

Step 5

On the third beat, the boy slides his left foot next to his right foot and stands with his feet together. The girl slides her right foot next to her left foot and stands with her feet together.

Step 6

For the next set of three beats, the boy starts with his right foot and the girl starts with her left foot. On the first beat, the boy takes a sliding step forward with his right foot. At the same time, the girl takes a sliding step back with her left foot.

Step 7

On the second beat, the boy slides forward and to the left with his left foot. At the same time, the girl slides backward and to the right with her right foot.

Step 8

Keep your feet in the spots where they are after the second beat. In between the second and third beats, the boy moves his weight from his right foot to his left. The girl moves her weight from her left foot to her right.

Step 9

On the third beat, the boy slides his right foot next to his left foot and stands feet together. The girl slides her left foot next to her right foot and stands feet together.

Step 10

Repeat these steps as you move gracefully to the music. While you are still learning, it sometimes helps to say the beat as you dance, ONE-two-three, ONE-two-three, ONE-two-three, and so on.

The Waltz King

Johann Strauss Jr. (1825–1899) was a classical music **composer** from Vienna, Austria. He is famous for all the waltz music he wrote. Strauss wrote more than 170 waltzes, beginning when he was only six years old! His most well-known waltzes include "The Blue Danube," "Tales from the Vienna Woods," and "The Emperor Waltzes."

CLEF NOTES

You can find a waltz beat in almost any kind of music, not just classical. Anytime you hear a song with a ONE-two-three beat, you can dance the waltz. Listen for this three-step count in rock, country, or **jazz** music. You'll be surprised where this familiar rhythm turns up!

Johann Strauss Jr.

Stage Your Own
OPERA

Materials Needed

- a story that already is or could be set to music
- instrumental music as a background for the singing
- as many performers as it will take to tell the story of your opera
- a stage or a similar place to put on your show
- a set, or background scenery
- costumes
- props
- an audience!

Operas were first performed in Italy in the 1500s. The earliest operas retold Greek legends. Audiences loved this form of musical storytelling. The operas had fancy stage designs, beautiful costumes, and famous singers. Today opera fans enjoy performances of many of these same productions!

Step 1

Decide what your opera is going to be about. You can write something new to perform. Or, you can perform a scene or two from an existing opera. You could sing the music yourself or lip-sync in character to a recording of an opera.

Step 2

Design and create the set. Where and when does the action of your opera take place? Create a stage design that shows both of these important parts of your opera. This will help your audience better understand and appreciate the story you're trying to tell.

Step 3

Design the costumes. Each performer in your opera will need a costume to match his or her role. Like the stage set, characters' costumes help an audience better understand and enjoy the story of an opera.

Step 4

Rehearse your performance. An opera includes singing and acting, so practice both. First practice the singing and acting separately, then put them together.

Step 5

Advertise your performance. Put up signs or make announcements that tell when, where, and what your performance will be. Otherwise, your audience might be rather small.

Step 6

Perform your opera in front of an audience. Get into it and have fun! If you and the other cast members enjoy yourselves and give your best effort, your audience will enjoy the performance too. Bravo! Bravo!

The ABCs of Opera

Aïda (by Giuseppe Verdi, 1813–1901). The pharaoh's daughter loves Radames, the captain of the Egyptian guards. But he is in love with Aïda, who is one of the pharaoh's slaves. When the pharaoh's daughter finds out Radames doesn't love her, she arranges for him to get in trouble.

The pharaoh sentences the captain to be buried alive. Aïda gives up her chance to escape slavery and instead returns to Radames. After they are sealed in a tomb, they die in each other's arms.

La Bohème (by Giacomo Puccini, 1858–1924). In 1830, four poor friends share a small apartment in Paris. Rodolfo, a poet, falls in love with Mimi and wants to live with her. The four roommates argue and go their separate ways.

But in a few months, they find themselves back together again. Then Mimi becomes deathly ill, and the four work together to save her. But it is too late. Mimi dies, and Rodolfo is heartbroken.

Carmen (by Georges Bizet, 1838–1875). In 1820 in Seville, Spain, a soldier named Don José is engaged to marry Micaela. But he meets and falls in love with a woman named Carmen. They run away together and Micaela finds them.

Don José leaves Carmen to go to his dying mother. Carmen then gives her love to another man. Don José finds out and gets very jealous, begging Carmen to come back to him. When she won't, he kills her.

Conclusion

Whether you are a fan of classical music or not, you can find something in it that will inspire you. It might be a particular piece of music. It might be the music of a certain **composer**. It might be the power and passion of musicians performing together in perfect harmony. It might be the heartbreaking drama of an opera.

Maybe you haven't found your connection to classical music yet. Keep an open mind and keep listening. It's there. You'll know it when you hear it.

And, you can do more than just listen to classical music, you can perform it! Many schools have bands and **orchestras**. Some cities also have youth orchestras or municipal bands.

If you prefer singing, join the school chorus or a youth choir. Get acting experience in school plays, children's theater, or community theater productions. If you want to make classical music, go for it!

Glossary

acoustics – the properties of a room that affect how sound is heard in it.

anthem – a song of gladness or patriotism.

audiophile – a person who is very enthusiastic about listening to recorded music.

composer – a person who writes music.

concert – a performance by musicians or singers.

copyright – the legal right to copy, sell, publish, or distribute the work of a writer, musician, or artist.

diameter - the distance across the middle of an object, such as a circle.

ensemble – a group of people working together on one performance or project.

folk – made by or traditional with the common people of an area.

genre – a category of art, music, or literature.

jazz – a style of music characterized by complex rhythms and melodies and improvised solos.

lyrics – the words of a song.

orchestra – a large group of musicians playing mostly stringed instruments together.

percussion – an instrument played by hitting, shaking, or striking it.

symphony – a long and complex piece of music to be played by an orchestra. A symphony orchestra plays symphonic music.

tempo – the speed at which a piece of music is to be played.

woodwind – a musical instrument made out of a tube of wood or metal that is played by blowing across a mouth hole or into a mouthpiece that contains one or two reeds.

Web Sites

To learn more about cool music, visit ABDO Publishing Company on the World Wide Web at **www.abdopublishing.com**. Web sites about cool music are featured on our Book Links pages. These links are routinely monitored and updated to provide the most current information available.

Index